THE PRACTICAL CHILD
DEVELOP WITH CONFIDENCE

First Published in 2021 by The Practical Child
www.thepracticalchild.com

Special thanks to Jane Hills-Kinsella for help, support and excellent rhyming skills

Dinosaurs

For Archer,
may your love of Dinosaurs never end!
xxx

Notes for Adults

This book has been designed by the Practical Child to help develop children's gross motor, fine motor and sensory skills. You will not need any equipment, meaning you can read the book and complete the activities anywhere.

Sally Hills-Davis is a childrens Occupational Therapist and Kirsty Brocklehurst is a childrens Physiotherapist, both highly specialised in child development

Ensure that children are supervised by an appropriate adult, whilst acting out the activities in this book. It is your responsibility to make sure the environment and activities are safe and suitable for your child.

This book has been designed for typically developing children. If your child has a medical condition or diagnosis, please consult with a health care professional before completing any of the activities in the book.

The activities in this book are designed to work on specific skills of child development:

Listening to the poems and following the instructions in the story will help work on the skills of listening, language and concentration.

 Listening

 Language

 Concentration

Visual perception refers to the brain's ability to make sense of what it is seeing. Hunting for the hidden item on each page helps this skill to develop.

Motor planning refers to the thought process behind making a series of organised movements

Each activity also focuses on developing one or more of the following key skills:

 Fine motor skills

 Balance

 Body Awareness

 Numeracy

 Hand eye Co-ordination

 Muscle strength

 Speech Production

 Sensory Processing

 Co-ordination

 Crossing midline

Look out for these symbols throughout the book

Stegosaurus
in herds they crawl,
spikes on their back
make them extra tall.

Action:
Crawl around on your hands
and knees like a Stegosaurus.

What do you think their skin felt like?

Diplodocus
is a gentle beast,
in a lagoon
is where they feast.

Action:

Balance on your tip toes and reach up with your arms to be as tall as a Diplodocus.

Can you describe what the Diplodocus looked like?

Triceratops have three horns on their head, watch out for where their big feet tread.

Action:

Point with your index fingers then put your hands on your head like Triceratops horns. Gently and slowly sway your head from side to side.

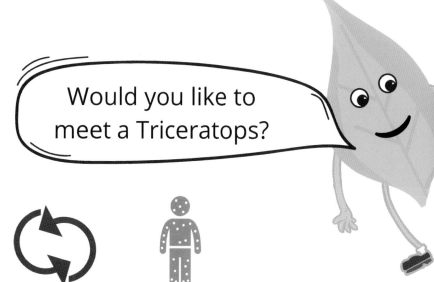

Would you like to meet a Triceratops?

Stomp like Ceratosaurus who likes to be alone, they have very big jaws to chew meat and bone.

Action:

Stomp around like a Ceratosaurus opening and closing your mouth wide and give a big roar!

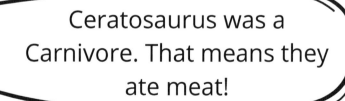

Ceratosaurus was a Carnivore. That means they ate meat!

Whilst strictly not one of the Dinosaurs, ruling the skies are the massive Pterosaurs.

Action:

Flap your arms and squawk like a Pterosaur flying through the sky.

The biggest Pterosaur had a wingspan of almost 16 metres! That's longer than a bus!

 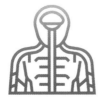  

Velociraptors hunt in packs, sharp claws grab tasty snacks.

Action:

Hook your finger out like a raptor claw,
try to jump on the spot 5 times.

Like this!

How many Velociraptors can you count?

Parasauralophus honks and eats leaves, they travel in herds through the trees.

Action:

Cup your hands around your mouth and honk like a Parasauralophus

Did you know that scientists do not know what colour dinosaurs were!

 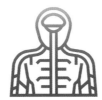 

Deinosuchus
has big teeth and snappy jaws, lurking in the water hiding razor sharp claws.

Action:

Keeping your elbows straight, open and snap close your arms like the Deinosuchus's mouth.

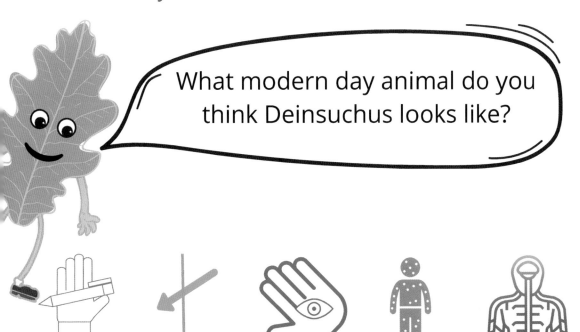

What modern day animal do you think Deinsuchus looks like?

Brachiosaurus babies hatching from their eggs, breaking out of their shell with their big strong legs.

Action:

Curl up into a tight ball and then slowly hatch out like a baby Brachiosaurus coming out of its shell.

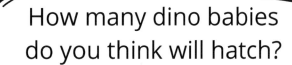

How many dino babies do you think will hatch?

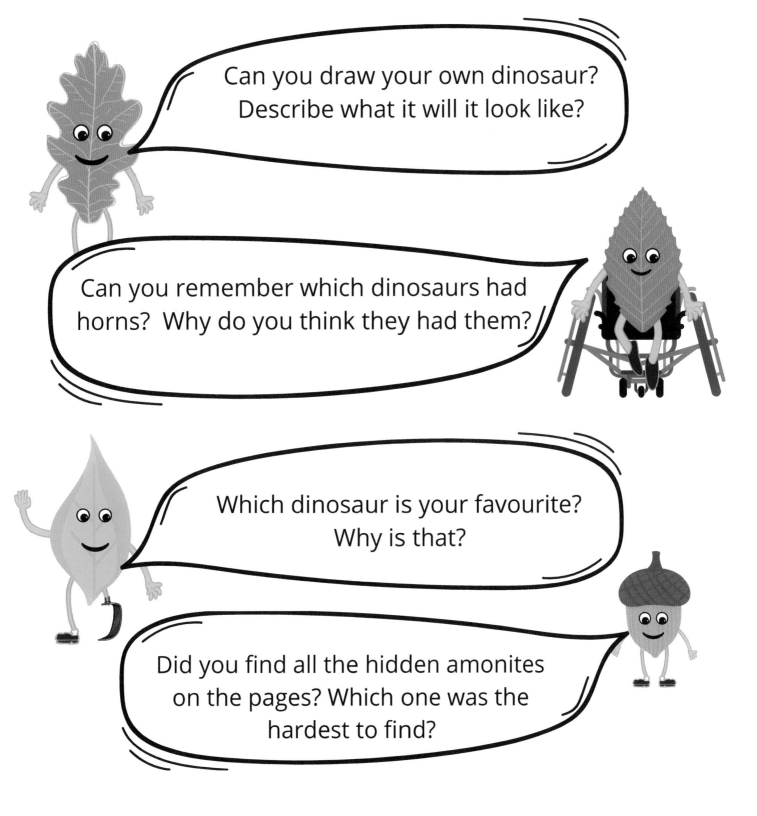

Can you help the mummy Brachiosaurus find her way back to her nest?

Ideas for Sensory Play

We have added this page to help give you and your children some ideas to get messy! Sensory play offers many additional experiences; we all respond to what we touch, move, see, hear, taste and smell. However, in a world where more and more green spaces and play areas are disappearing, the opportunities to get messy are not always available to us.

Ideas:

- Make up some playdough (download the recipe from **The Making Series** at www.thepracticalchild.com) colouring it brown. Make giant foot prints.

- Make mud out of cocoa powder and water

- Make a forest with leaves and sticks on a tray. Fill a bowl with water for a lake for the dinosaurs to come and drink from

- Make a stomping sound on the ground to tell the children that the dinosaurs are on the way (obviously not scaring your child but making it fun)

Ensure that children are supervised by an appropriate adult, at all times. It is your responsibility to make sure the props used are safe and suitable.

Visit www.thepracticalchild.com for more tips and advice on child development, training packages and to see more books from the READ, DO, DEVELOP series.

THE PRACTICAL CHILD
DEVELOP WITH CONFIDENCE

Find us on

www.thepracticalchild.com

READ, DO, DEVELOP

More books available in the Read Do Develop series:

For younger children try our Read Do Develop Mini series suitable from birth

All avaliable from www.thepracticalchild.com